Evolution of a Frightened Child into a Serial Killer

The Childhood and Adult Psychological Evaluations

Robert M. Dowling, Ph.D.

Deldon Publishing

To those I love: VV, KE, RD, JS, TP, MJ, SM.

"... I have uncovered the transparent monsters who had tramped across my path-my serial killers-while you perhaps have not uncovered yours. I pray you never will."

—Peter Vronsky in <u>*Serial Killer*</u>

~~~

I share this prayer with my readers as well.

—*RMD<u>s</u>*

AUTHOR'S NOTE: This book is written primarily for professional psychologists. However, those interested in criminology, the phenomenon of serial murderers, or behavioral deviation in general should also find it of interest. A knowledge of psychological evaluation, especially the Rorschach Ink Blots, would be helpful but is not necessary.

TABLE OF CONTENTS

I

———✴———

INTRODUCTION

In 1962 I was employed as a psychologist at the DePaul Clinic in Rochester, New York. There I had the task of evaluating an eleven year-old boy. He was referred for problems with facial tics and day-time enuresis. Seventeen years later, in 1979, he again came to my attention by way of a phone call from a criminal defense attorney. The attorney's client had been accused of murdering two young women in Bellingham, Washington. He was also suspected of being involved in the brutal murders of at least ten other young females in Los Angeles in collusion with his cousin.

The client was Kenneth Bianchi, the young preadolescent I had seen at DePaul Clinic. He was subsequently found guilty of the Bellingham murders as well as some of those attributed to the Hillside Stranglers in Los Angeles.

The attorney, Mr. Dean Brett, was in the process of gathering information about his client and had received the medical records from the DePaul Clinic. He sent these to me for review. We had several telephone conversations and exchanged correspondence regarding Kenneth Bianchi..

My interest in this case continued as it came to involve a possible insanity defense based on the diagnosis of multiple personality. The pretrial investigation involved psychological and psychiatric evaluations. I was able to obtain all of the psychological tests completed at that time. They are all part of the public record. (see Appendix A for a letter from Attorney Brett).

In subsequent chapters I will include all of the psychological evaluation data collected at ages eleven and twenty-seven. Selected information from the social history will also be presented. More complete historical details can be found in the copious articles on the internet as well as in the well documented books by Ted Schwarz (*The Hillside Strangler)* and Darcy O'Brien (*Two of a Kind* also published as *The Hillside Stranglers).*

All of the information herein, that is not in the public record, is taken from these sources. A book by Naomi Roberts (also titled *The Hillside Stranglers)* provides additional data about both of the "Stranglers" as well as information regarding television and movies dealing with the case.

I decided to write this book after these many years for several reasons. I always thought this story should be told - not Kenneth Bianchi's story - but the story of his psychological and psychiatric evaluations. I considered it important that all of the test results at both ages be available some place in the psychological literature. I know of no other serial killer who has been evaluated as a child and as an adult. In Peter Vronsky's well researched and comprehensive book, *Serial Killers,* there is no mention of any of them being psychologically evaluated at two different ages. Most studies by psychologists of serial killers tend to make a comparison of them to single or mass murderers, to psychopaths or to other kind of psychopathological conditions. For example, the journal *Behavioral Sciences & the Law* published in 2004 an issue devoted exclusively to "Serial and Mass Homicides." It included three articles comparing singular and serial offenses, one dealing with serial murders by children and adolescent and a case study of seven serial murderers.

I also thought it important that the results of a study conducted by Dr. Susan Hamilton and myself get into the psychological literature. In it we compare the two Rorschach Ink Blots tests taken by Kenneth Bianchi at ages eleven and twenty-seven. A synopsis of this study is found in Chapter 4.

II

SELECTED SOCIAL HISTORY

CHILDHOOD

The DePAUL Clinic Data

The DePaul Clinic was a typical child guidance clinic of the time. It was staffed by psychiatric social workers, a psychologist, and directed by a psychiatrist. The Clinic provided mental health services to the parochial schools of the Diocese of Rochester, New York.

Upon referral of a chid the procedure was for the social worker to interview the parents. The child would subsequently be seen individually by the psychologist and the psychiatrist. A diagnostic conference would then be held and a plan of treatment determined.

The Social Worker Notes

Rather then attempt to summarize these I will selectively quote from his written notes:

5/1/62 Mother called saying that the boy wets his pants and has a prostate gland problem … Mother sounded anxious and felt that Kenneth was afraid of his teacher.

5/12/62 I telephoned mother and gave her an appointment for 6/2/62 at 10 a.m.

6/2/62 Mother did not come in at 10 a.m. but came in at 3 P.M. … claimed I gave her an appointment for 3 P.M. … She impressed me as an upset woman who was quite hostile … made an appointment for 6/9/62.

6/9/62 Mrs. Bianchi came in accompanied by her husband … she didn't think the boy needed to come here but she was sick and tired of people telling her that he needed see a psychiatrist … other children laugh at him and if necessary, she would get a lawyer … she seemed extremely upset … she is obviously the dominant one in the family … (husband) sat meekly by, hardly saying anything … Mrs. Bianchi talked for over an hour with my hardly being able to say anything … Kenneth was adopted … when he was 3 months old, this was a private adoption … in the 2nd grade mother found that the boy was constantly dripping urine … (she) became very agitated and insisted that the boy be hospitalized (this ended in an argument with the hospital staff and with Kenneth being removed before any treatment) … When I asked mother to sign a release form she said she would not sign until after she had an opportunity to tell me her complete story.

Child.s problems: The boy drips urine … doesn't make friends very easily and has twitches … other children make fun of him and mother is extremely angry at the school because they do not stop the other children. Mother sounds … very overprotective … When the boy fell on the playground in kindergarten early in the school year, she kept him home the total year.

Impressions: ... this boy sounds as if he does have some emotional problems. The mother, is obviously, very emotionally disturbed at this point.

7/18/62 On returning from vacation I received a note that Mrs. Bianchi had called on 7/10/62, and was rather upset. When I reached her she said she called ... and was pretty upset because Kenneth was wetting his pants more ... she didn't take him to Dr. T. because he told them to go to a psychiatrist ... she took him to (another physician). Obviously, mother is still following her same pattern of going from one doctor to another in dissatisfaction.

7/21/62 Mother noted the face twitching at age 5 ... She recalled that the child fell from the top of playground bars and ... wonders if he did not injure some nerves ... because of this she feels he is nervous ... Mother is concerned that the child is getting freckles (which) are turning into moles and the doctor doesn't think this is serious ... is frustrated in not getting a better answer from the doctor (she) talked about herself as being nervous and coming from a nervous family ... when she got nervous she used to imagine she had all kinds of ailments ... she said that she was crying a great deal and recently went to see a psychiatrist herself ... she would not give me the name of the psychiatrist ... I pointed out that she seemed to be holding back information ... (and) it was important enough to know what concerned her and what she has attempted to do about these things.

IMPRESSION: ... when I focused on Kenneth, Mrs. Bianchi almost resented this and wanted someone to listen to her.

7/28/62 She brought along a very complete resume of the boy"s life, accompanied by a multitude of pictures of his various stages of development ... Mrs. Bianchi is a very controlling woman who attempts to get her way by being bombastic ... She constantly projects the cause of her difficulty on to others and I feel she is doing the same with Kenneth.

Kenneth was seen by me on 10/16/62 and 11/6/62 for the purpose of performing the psychological evaluation. As the result of misunderstandings about appointment times Kenneth was not seen by the psychiatrist until January 22nd and 30th of 1963.

A diagnostic conference was held on March 21, 1963. (The psychological report and psychiatric observation and diagnosis are presented on separate pages.)

The Social Worker Notes

3/21/63 (At the diagnostic conference) it was recommended that this boy have individual or group psychotherapy and his mother be seen in casework ... we could not start the boy immediately because of a time problem but that the mother ... should begin as soon as possible ... possibly weekly and have the boy seen once per month while on the (treatment) waiting list.

April 6, 1963 I saw Mr. and Mrs. Bianchi in an interpretive interview ... (I told them) we saw (Kenneth) as a tense, anxious boy ... (they were) surprisingly receptive ... Mother seemed to have some awareness that the boy had been very close to her ... appointments were set up for Mr. Bianchi on 4/24/63 and Mrs. Bianchi on 4/27/63.

April 24, 1963 ... someone called and said (Mr. Bianchi) would not be able to come.

April 27, 1963 I telephoned Mrs.Bianchi who said ... she would not be able to keep her appointment today because she is not feeling well ... she said that she would call me for another appointment.

June 22, 1963 I had not heard from Mrs. Bianchi ... I called her ... she told me that things had improved a lot ... his nervous condition has not come back so far ... she didn't see any need for further appointments ... and would call ... if she wanted further help ... we can consider this case closed as of 6/22/1963.

Almost three years later on March 25, 1966 Mrs. Bianchi came to the Clinic unannounced and was seen briefly by Dr. Sullivan. He advised her that the Clinic would call to set up an appointment. She was seen on April 26 by a different psychiatric social worker. Mrs. Bianchi's concerns at that time centered around Kenneth's school difficulties (he was failing five subjects), his lack of emotional reaction to his father's sudden death, and his "interest in sexual matters." She impressed this new social worker "as a rather provocative woman who is having some problems herself with an adolescent son." She wanted Ken to be seen at the Clinic but when told that she would also need to be involved, "she retreated from her position." She said she "would think this matter over" and let me know. "Since we haven't heard from Mrs. Bianchi or Ken, I am considering this one appointment as a consultation effort with Mrs. Bianchi and the case remains closed."

<u>PSYCHOLOGICAL REPORT</u>

BIANCHI, Kenneth   Age: 11.4   Seen: 10-16-62, 11-6-62

<u>Tests Administered</u>: WISC (vocabulary subtest only), Bender-Gestalt,
Figure Drawings, Rhode Sentence Completion Test,
Rorschach

Kenneth was a fidgity, somewhat feminine appearing boy who was very eager
to relate to the examiner. He did so, however, only with considerable
strain and discomfort, exhibiting many twitches of his face and upper
extremities. He denied knowing why he was coming to the Clinic but
thought that it had something to do with his school work. His cooperation
with the test demands approached subserviance.

Kenneth is a very anxious and lonely boy who appears to live under the
constant threat that "she" (this is his usual way of referring to his
mother) will withdraw her support from him. It would appear from
Kenneth's viewpoint that his mother has related to him in such a way
so that he feels his very survival depends on his being in her good
graces. In order to do so, he must maintain very rigid control over
his masculine aggressive impulses. He accomplishes this through the
use of severe repression, primitive denial and obsessive-compulsive
constrictive techniques. The need not to show any masculine assertiveness
is so great that his basic identification is quite diffuse and contains
as much of a feminine component as a masculine one. The latter, however,
is seen as the more basic aspect so that the former is used to cover-up
those aspects of his masculinity that are unacceptable to his mother.
It would appear that the self-assertive, aggressive, dominating tendencies
of the male greatly displease Mrs. Bianchi for it is these that Kenneth
expends so much energy keeping in rigid control. This is extremely
anxiety provoking for him because it is his mother, who by her controlling
relationship with him, stimulates his hostility. There is a tremendous
amount of anxiety generated in all of this, so much so that one wonders
how well Kenneth could maintain his psychological integrity if he did not
somatocize it in the way that he does. His physical complaints have a
large anxiety component and he uses them to express indirectly some of
the hostility towards his mother that he harbors.

In summary, Kenneth is a boy of estimated Bright-Normal intelligence who is
very lonely and extremely anxious. He is living in an intensely patho-
logical relationship with his mother which is seriously hampering his
psycyological development. Not only are his identification and self-
concept shaken by this mode of life but his behavior is so defensively
oriented that little energy is left over for constructive pursuits. He
appears to have a spark of creativity but it is doubtful that he will be
able to utilize this because of the constriction he must maintain over
his self-expression, except perhaps in the service of his own defensive

---

BIANCHI, Kenneth   -2-

fantasies. It is thought that Kenneth would respond well to individual
psychotherapy but without simultaneous treatment of his mother, who
it appears is not accepting of such a plan, the effects of such a
course of action would be fleeting.

                                 R. M. Dowling, Ph.D.
                                 Clinical Psychologist

Abc

BIANCHI, Kenneth

This 11½ year old boy is in the 5th grade and was referred by the school because of absenteeism, tics, enuresis, asthma, and many behavior problems.

The boy was adopted privately in an arrangement between his mother and the adoptive mother.

Father is 43 and is said to be dominated by his wife. He is said to be phobic about worms and insects and has a speech defect. He is said to have an 11th grade education.

The adoptive mother also has an 11th grade education and is a very tense, hostile, labile woman who takes tranquilizers. She has been very hostile towards hospitals, doctors, nurses and others who have been responsible for the boy's medical care. She feels the doctors don't understand her. She stated that she would never let a man get the best of her. She has been seen by other agencies where the impression was that she was a deeply disturbed woman who was socially ambitious, opiniated, over-protective, controlling and guilt-ridden regarding the child. She had a hysterectomy in 1951, which was followed by some depression.

PAST HISTORY:
The boy's natural mother was said to be a barmaid who the adoptive mother considers to be "oversexed". Nothing is known about the birth history.

In the first few months of his life, he lived in foster homes with an allegedly alcoholic foster mother. When he was 3 months old, he was adopted and at that time he was allegedly very sick..vomiting and needed considerable care. Very quickly he began eating well and gained weight. When he was 2½ years old, the family went to California where they sought psychiatric help for him. He stayed for 4½ years. Apparently, he had "throat asthma" while there. When he was 4 years old, he had a fall, and began rolling his eyes in an episode that sounded like a petit mal attack. When he was 5 years old, he began having tics including facial movements and throat clearing. Medical attention was sought and no organic illness was seen. In 1958, the family was known at Northside Hospital service, social; in 1959, known at SPCC, complaint was the boy was not being properly cared for. He was seen briefly this year at the Psychiatric Clinic at Strong. Mother apparently was unwilling to continue this contact.

When he was 7½ years old, 2 foster children were taken into the home, within a month and a month later were removed. He then began having enuresis and the tics got worse.

10

In 1958, he was studied at Northside Hospital for enuresis and was found to have a horseshoe kidney. On admission, the mother was found to be quite hostile towards physician who suggested he did not have a physical cause for his enuresis but had emotional disturbance. Mother complained of his being neglected and the mother said the boy told her this and she believed it because he'd been "whipped" when he lies, so he won't lie to her. Mother's insistence on organicity resulted in conflict and he was discharged against advice.

OBSERVATION OF KENNETH
Seen: 1/22/63, 1/30/63

Kenneth is a well developed, slender, healthy appearing, attractive boy with a mild overbite. His speech is adequate.

He was anxious, passive, cooperative, conforming and easily threatened. He covers his anxiety and his lack of confidence. He appears to be a rather lonely boy who clings to home rather than face the dangers of the outside world. He is easily threatened, fears authority and aggressive people whom he tries to pacify.

About himself, he said he has a horseshoe kidney which makes him wet his pants some time, but he is getting over it. He is nervous most of the time, particularly when he gets excited in play or someone hollers at him. He feels sad when there is no one to play with. He revealed his fear of adults; particularly with aggressive people. He doesn't know what he wants to be when he grows up but his wishes were that there would be no more school, that he wouldn't have to work hard, that he could live forever and he would enjoy life more. His fun is putting on scary plays with his boyfriends in which he is the monster. Mother sometimes watches; father does not. He was hospitalized 3 times, but he couldn't remember why. He didn't like hospitals because he had to go to bed early.

He said he hates school because it is hard and the teacher yells at him. He went on to say that the teacher shouldn't "take it out on other kids". He said that the children sometimes blame him for doing things that he hadn't done and the teacher believes it so he gets blamed. He gets nervous when he has to do school work and is not able to do it.

He said his mother will do anything to help him, even if she is sick. She hollers a great deal and is the boss. She does the punishing. He developed facial tics talking about his mother. He said she bosses his father who does what she says.

He indicated his father is nice and helpful and doesn't get angry at him.

Drawing of a person was a very mature detailed drawing of a policeman.

11

It showed good intelligence and good body image concept.

FORMULATION:
This is a phobic boy with many counterphobias. He uses repression
and reaction formation. He is an only child adopted by a rather
passive man who is dominated by his rather emotionally labile wife
who appears to have considerable drive and masculine protest. Hysterical
acting out and projective tendencies were strongly suggested from the
history.

She has dominated the boy and indulged him in terms of her own needs.
Her anxious, protective, clinging control has made him ambivalent but
he represses the hostile aggression and is increasingly dependent upon
her. He resolves this ambivalence through phobic behavior. He also
has pregenital conversions as mentioned.

Apparently the absenteeism from school is related to his separation
difficulty due to the school phobia. His mother will not accept an
emotional basis for this and the blame is projected to his teacher.
He also has regressive behavior such as diurnal and nocturnal enuresis
at times.

The boy is very lonely and has been kept from adequate peer relationships.

DIAGNOSIS:
Personality trait disturbance, other.
Psychoneurosis, phobic reaction and anxiety.

RECOMMENDATION:
Because of the mother's threat of authority and her counterphobic behavior
of defying authority, casework may be difficult. It should be directed
towards supporting her and recognizing that she has had some difficulties
in raising this boy and having her needs understood.

The boy might benefit from group therapy or individual therapy.

Follow-up is indicated in March 1963.

                                        A. W. Sullivan, M.D.

Abc

12

ADULTHOOD

Rochester, New York

Mrs. Bianchi's concerns about her son, as expressed during her last visit to DePaul Clinic, were both accurate and inaccurate. She was correct that he had failing grades in the Catholic school he was attending but he was able to change schools and was successfully graduated. He enrolled at a community college to become a police officer (a continuing desire of his) but soon dropped out.

Contrarily, her worry about his failure to express any emotion over his father's sudden death was apparently unfounded. Father and son had begun to do more things together such as taking fishing trips. They had become somewhat close and Kenneth was both surprised and pleased to learn that they both wore the same size shoe. He was 13 years old at the time of his father's passing and expressed his sorrow in appropriate ways, but in ways not obvious to his mother.

In his young adult years he was apparently eager to settle down and get married. At age 18 he proposed to a girl who turned him down. He soon married a young woman but that was short lived. At age 20 he married again but, as before, this did not last long as his wife left him after eight months.

His job seeking efforts were similarly disappointing. Continuing with his penchant for police work, he applied for a position with the sheriff's office but was turned down. He eventually found related work as a security guard. However, he was eventually fired due to being suspected of petty thievery by his fellow employees.

In January of 1976, at age 25, he decided to leave Rochester. He had an older cousin who lived in Los Angeles, who he had visited as a child. So, with that connection, he chose Los Angeles as his destination.

Los Angeles, California

The cousin, 44 year old Angelo Buono, was street wise, to say the least. He was well known among certain prostitutes and introduced his young cousin to that side of the L.A. scene. The pair of cousins got along well and developed a good relationship but Buono was always the "boss", the *capo*.

Bianchi was also busy with his own life. He applied to the Los Angeles Police Reserves and was accepted; he found employment as a clerk with a land title company. There he met an attractive woman. The attraction was mutual and they eventually moved in together. He wanted to get married; she wanted to wait.

Bianchi was a good "lover" but a poor "husband". He would do nice things for her such as write her poetry and bring her flowers and other gifts (many of which he had stolen). At the same time, however, he showed little development in maturity. He was financially irresponsible in many ways including once having a car repossessed. He would also miss work explaining to his employer that he had "cancer treatment appointments", which was not true. He also greatly enjoyed staying out late with his cousin, "playing cards."

The relationship between Bianchi and his girl friend continued to vacillate but eventually it became too stressful for her. In March of 1978 she left him and returned to her parent's home in Bellingham, Washington.

Meanwhile the "card playing" had become something very different. Cousin Angelo quickly introduced Bianchi to the practice of "pimping" an activity which he seemed to enjoy, especially the rougher side of it.

Perhaps the first murder was a punishment "gone wrong." The victim was a prostitute who had played a trick on Bianchi and Buono by providing them a false list of potential prostitution clients. But even before then, the two of them had already discussed the notion of killing women. Either way, the rampage began.

The two of them, working together, brutally tortured, sodomized, raped and strangled ten females, ranging in age from twelve to twenty-eight. They displayed their work for all the world to see by placing their mutilated, naked bodies on various hillsides throughout the area.

The victims:

1. Yolanda M., age 19, a prostitute and a mother;

2. Judith M., age 15, a runaway;

3. Lissa K., age 21, a waitress;

4. Jane K., age 28, an aspiring actress;

5. Sonia J., age 14, friend of Dollie C., abducted together;

6. Dollie C., age 12, friend of Sonia J., abducted together;

7. Kristina W., age 20, a college student;

8. Lauren W., age 18, a high school student;

9. Kimberly M., age 18, a call girl;

10. Cindy H., age 20, a college student.

Although Buono was the elder and perhaps the original instigator, the younger man was equally involved in all of the murders. Bianchi used his good looks and approachable manner to entice them into the car or his Police Reserve badge to frighten them. Once involved, he experimented with various means of torture and carried out some of the strangulations. These ten murders took place during the five months between October of 1977 and February of 1978 (twice as many as Jack the Ripper in about the same amount of time). A task force of police from the different cities involved were working diligently but seemingly not making much progress. They talked to Bianchi more than once because one of the victims lived in his neighborhood. However, they did not consider him a suspect. During this same time period he had also accompanied the police on a "ride along" as a Reservist and asked if he could see the "Strangler" sites.

Bianchi, being a braggart and also in need of approval from his older cousin, told Buono how he had fooled the cops. This worried the older cousin who thought that sooner or later he was going to say too much to the wrong people. Buono wanted him to leave Los Angeles. But Bianchi insisted that he loved it there, even suggesting that they try another "pick up" - as if it were a "fun" thing they could do together. This only made Buono more insistent on his leaving. But Bianchi was family, an adoptive cousin, but still *famiglia*. Buono just couldn't abandon him.

Then Bianchi told him that his girl friend had left him and relocated in Bellingham, and Buono saw this as a solution to his problem. He first tried to talk Bianchi into joining her but Bianchi procrastinated. Buono eventually had to threaten to kill him if he didn't leave California.

Finally in May of 1978, taking his cousin at his word, Bianchi left L.A. for Bellingham.

Bellingham, Washington

Things went quite well initially for Bianchi in his new location. He was successful in "sweet talking" his girl friend into letting him move in with her.

He was actually quite good at talking his way into and out of various situations - didn't he talk the police into accepting him into the Reserve and also talk them out of considering him a suspect? He had frequently thought of using this skill "professionally" as a counselor. He, of course, didn't have the appropriate credentials so he set out to obtain them. He first placed an ad, under the name of Dr. R. Johnson, for an assistant. He asked potential candidates to forward their college transcripts to him. He received several responses and selected that of *Thomas Steven Walker* who had a Master of Arts degree in psychology from one of the California state universities. He then wrote to that institution, under the name of *Walker*, asking to receive "a full completed diploma EXCEPT for my name." He explained that he had hired a calligrapher to print his name in a "fancy script." He actually received a genuine diploma and forwarded it to the calligrapher. She, apparently, did such a poor job that he was unable to make use of it.

He moved on to other projects. (Documents concerning this event can be found in APPENDIX B.)

Bianchi applied for membership in the local county Sheriff's Reserve and was accepted. He began attending police procedure classes. He obtained employment as a non-uniformed floorwalker at a local store. He and his girl friend were getting along better than ever. Things were looking up. Things were also getting rather dull for him in this relatively small city. It was not what he had become accustomed to in L.A.

His reputation as a reliable floorwalker led to his obtaining a position with a security firm. Among the jobs this firm handled was checking on unoccupied homes while the owners were away. Doing this was one of Bianchi's responsibilities. The firm provided him with the title of "captain", a uniform, and a vehicle. Using these props he lured two Western Washington University coeds to an unoccupied house. He told them the house's alarm system was being repaired and promised them one hundred dollars for house sitting. Once they were inside, using a cord, he strangled both of the women. Their relatively intact bodies were found the next day. Bianchi was also arrested that same day. It was January 12, 1979

The Arrest and Its Aftermath

When the women were first reported as missing the police found in their rooms handwritten notes about the "house sitting job" that mentioned Bianchi's name. When they went to Bianchi's home they found jewelry that one of the women's parents identified as belonging to their daughter. When they went to Bianchi's employer he said there was no alarm system being repaired and the keys to the unoccupied house were missing. When they went to another of the firm's work sites they found Bianchi who claimed and acted as if had no idea why he was being accused of the two murders.

Using his California driver license the police made inquiries in Los Angeles. It was not long before they had enough information about him and his cousin to accuse them both of the Hillside Stranglers murders. Again, Bianchi claimed no knowledge or memory of any of these accusations.

This feigned amnesia by Bianchi was apparently very believable and the source of concern to both his attorney as well as the prosecuting attorney. His attorney, Mr. Bret, hired a psychiatric social worker to help Bianchi adjust to his sudden life changes. After several sessions with him the social worker suggested to Mr. Bret that perhaps Bianchi was suffering from a condition called multiple personality (now called dissociative reaction). A diagnosis in which a different personality takes control of the patient's behavior, for a period of time, without the original (the host) personalty's awareness.

Mr. Bret informed the presiding judge of his intention to pursue a defense of not guilty by reason of insanity. The judge, in turn, ordered the appointment of six mental health experts: two to be chosen by the prosecution; two by the defense; and two by the court.

These professionals included psychiatrists and psychologists. Some of them used hypnosis, a standard treatment for multiple personality disorder. The psychologists also administered a variety of psychological tests.

Also present were a group of detectives from Los Angeles. They were sure he was one of the Hillside Stranglers and they were very doubtful about his having amnesia for all of the killings.

Bianchi himself was apparently unsure himself that he would be successful faking being a multiple personality. He had tried several things to "throw off" the detectives. One of these involved writing to his mother. He enclosed a handwritten letter that implicated a boyfriend of one of the Bellingham's victims. He requested she fly from Rochester to Seattle and mail the note to the Bellingham police. She declined to do this for her son.

As mentioned, Bianchi was subjected to hypnoses. The purpose of this was to induce a trance in an attempt to get the "other" person to "come out" and to speak directly with "it" (not always of the same gender as the "host" personality). Bianchi had done some reading on hypnosis and may have tried it out as a parlor game among friends. He was very good at faking being in a trance state.

In one such state he successfully produced an adult young man as the "other" personality. And after a number of hypnotic sessions this personality admitted to most of the murders. Now the police knew they had the "hands" that did the killing. But whose "hands" were they? Were they the hands of the "other" or was Bianchi faking being hypnotized?

During one feigned hypnotic session Bianchi gave the "other" personality the name of *Steve Walker*. The detectives, when they listened to the recording of this session, recalled that Bianchi had used that name previously. A search of their records revealed it to be the name of the individual whose college transcript he had fraudulently obtained. It seemed to the detectives that to use this same name, when supposedly hypnotized, suggested that he was really faking the trance state.

People with the diagnosis of multiple personality disorder will frequently have names for their "other" personality but it is not usually the name of an actual person. The mental heath professionals confirmed the detectives' suspicion. Bianchi made several other "mistakes" while "hypnotized". After he was informed by one of the psychiatrist that most "multiples" usually have more than one "other" personalty, another one, named Billy, appeared at the next session. Also he once attempted to shake hands with an imagined person, something never observed in hypnotized subjects without the suggestion of the hypnotist.

Bianchi was exposed. He eventually admitted to the Bellingham murders as well as some of those in Los Angeles. The prosecution believed they needed his testimony in order to convict his accomplish so they made him an offer. This entailed life imprisonment instead of the death sentence. It also included the possibility of parole and Bianchi's agreement to testify against Angelo Buono in California. It was October 3, 1980.

Also part of the prosecution's offer was the agreement by California authorities to allow Bianchi to serve his sentence in that state's prison system rather than at the "tougher" Washington state prison at Walla Walla, Washington.

Angelo Buono was found guilty in the longest trial, until then, in California's history. Contributing to the length of the trail was Bianchi's poor testimony. This was so contradictory, ambiguous, and confusing that the trial judge ruled that he did not keep his end of the agreement. Bianchi was sent to Walla Walla. It was January 9, 1984.

Bianchi's psychiatric diagnosis: Antisocial personality disorder with sexual sadism.

III

THE PSYCHOLOGICAL EVALUATIONS

CHILDHOOD EVALUATION

I saw Kenneth on October 6, 1962 to conduct an interview and administered the following tests: the Vocabulary subtest from the Wechsler Intelligence Scale for Children, Bender Gestalt Test, and Figure Drawings. When seen again on November 16, 1962 Kenneth responded to the Rohde Sentence Completions and I administered the Rorschach Inkblots.

Interview

Dr.D. (greeting; How are you doing?)

    KB: So far so good.

(Do you know why you're here today?)

    I don't know.

(What do you think?)

    I don't know.

(What grade are you in?)

    Six.

(How are you doing?)

    Better then last year.

(What are your grades?)

    B's and C's.

(How are things at home?)

    Fine.

(What kind of things do you like to do?)

    Go play with my boy friends - we play war. I like to play touch football.

(Do you watch much TV?)

    Always.

(What do like to watch?)

    5 O'Clock Theater, the Early Show, some cartoons.

(Which ones?)

All of them and movies at night.

(Do you get to stay up late?)

I used to. Now I have to go to bed at eight o' clock.

(Do you dream much?)

About every night.

(What about?)

I forget.

(Any scary dreams?)

I used to but not any more.

(Did they wake you?)

Yeah.

(What did you do then?)

Fall back to sleep.

(What is the best thing that could happen to you?)

Getting what I always wanted.

(And what is that?)

A camping set.

(What is the worst thing?)

Have all my privileges taken away - and moving away from the neighborhood.

(What do you like to do?)

Watching TV, staying up past 8, going out after supper, bringing my boy friend in the house.

(Is he special?)

He's the only one allowed in the house.

(Do you have any girl friends?)

Yeah, two or three of them.

(When do you get to see them?)

Once in a while - sometimes when I go out to play.

(If you had three wishes, what would you wish for?)

One, I'd live where we live now for the rest of my life; two, have a lot of money to buy what I wanted or needed; and three, buy that camping set.

(Tell me about that.)

The Marine Raider Camping Set.

(What's in it?)

A tent, place for food, a canteen - it sells for seven dollars.

(Did you ask your Mom about it?)

She said, Whatever you get, be satisfied.

(How about your father?)

He told me to ask my mother.

(If you could be any kind of animal, for pretend, what kind of animal would you be?)

A bird.

(What would you do?)

> Fly all over 'cause you can't get hurt - just fly all around and get some food.

Wechsler Intelligence Scale for Children

I did not receive a copy of the Wechsler Intelligence Scale for Children from the attorney. My notes indicate he obtained a score of 116 which is in the High Average range at approximately the 85th percentile rank.

Bender Gestalt Test (see following two pages)

(I'm going to show you these cards one at a time and I want you to copy them on this paper for me.)

My notes taken during administration of the Bender Gestalt:

"no comment; rotates paper-throughout; #3 R to L; #7 top to bottom, but rotates paper so does both L to R, erasing; #8 erasing."

A second administration was given with the following instruction: "This time, hold the paper this way." This was done because he did not place them in the order in which they were presented - which most people at any age usually do.

Notes: "no comment; counting; #3 erasing and counting."

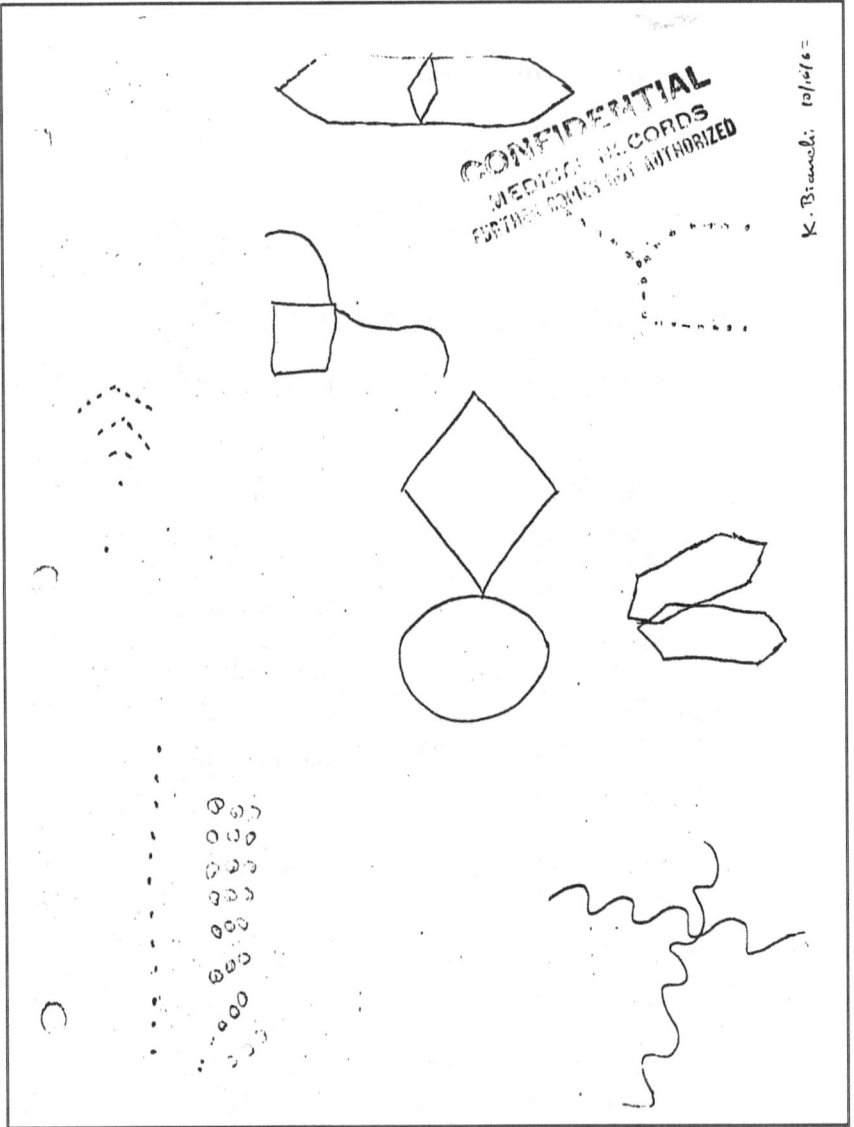

K. Bianchi. 10/10/6=

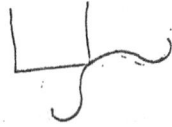

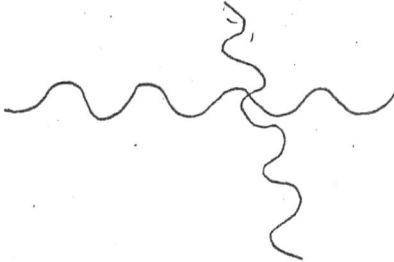

10/16/62
I copy
Kenneth B

Draw-a-Person (see following two pages)

(Now I would like you to draw a picture of a person.)

Any kind?

(Yes, any kind.)

Notes taken during drawing #I: "Starts with what looks like a hat then erases, spends a lot time and energy on head and hat, then to neck & trunk, had two pockets on shirt then erased one, then both, buttons, pockets back on, then hands, legs & feet, then pockets in pants, club at side."

(Now draw a picture of the opposite sex.)

(no comment)

Notes taken during drawing #II: "starts with shoulder straps on dress, then to dress & arms, working much faster then above, then hands - erases hands, to facial features - hair, then hands with gloves, then decoration on dress, shades in dress."

Interview after both drawings were completed:

Drawing #I

(Who is he?)

A policeman.

(What is he doing.)

Walking - taking a walk.

(What made you think of that?)

It just came into my mind.

(What do you think is best about it?)

The jacket.

(The worst?)

The feet.

Drawing #II

(Who is she?)

Just some singer - a dancer or a singer in a night club.

(What is she doing?)

Just standing and singing a song.

(What is the best about it?)

The dress.

(The worst?)

The hair.

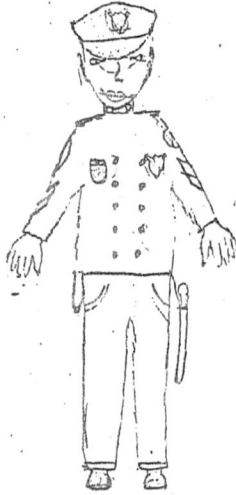

31

Rohde Sentence Completions

ROHDE SENTENCE COMPLETIONS

by

AMANDA R. ROHDE

K. Bianchi

Published by

WPS
Established 1948

WESTERN PSYCHOLOGICAL SERVICES
PUBLISHERS • DISTRIBUTORS • CONSULTANTS
BOX 775, BEVERLY HILLS, CALIFORNIA

In the accompanying exercises you will find a number of sentences to complete like the following:

1. Some people_____

2. Playing games_____

Date_____   Sex_____

Kindly complete the following sentences as rapidly as possible.

1. My schoolwork _is awfully hard._

2. The future _is far away._

✓3. I want to know _if I am going to get a marine raider se_

4. Our family _is a happy family._

5. I feel _fine today._

6. The training _I get at home is very good._

7. Much of the time _I am in school._

8. Money often _is hard to get_

✓9. If I _get the marine raider camping set_ (soon?) _I won't a for anythi._

10. Working _hard is the_ (?) _learning._

11. I suffer _very little._

12. Friends _like me._

✓13. My mother _is the best mother in the whole world_

14. There are times _when the going gets ruff._

15. Eating _is the number 1 thing to health._

16. My mind _is always busy._

17. I sleep _from 10 to 11 hours every nite._

✓18. My greatest longing _is friends._

19. God _is the greatest person of all_

20. My imagination _is awfully imaginary._

21. Most boys (men) _are smarter than girls (women)._

22. My clothes _are very nice._

23. The laws we have _are very good._

24. I fear _going to the doctor or dentist._

✓25. My greatest trouble _is getting my mother or father to by me that marine raider camping set it scars were we where the other day._

33

26. Earning my living _I don't have to do._
27. Many of my dreams _are very good._
28. Secretly I _think that I'm going to get what I want!_ _christin_
29. My stomach _is all right._
30. I cannot understand what makes me _nervous._

31. Most people _are so nice._
32. My father _is the very best father in the whole world_
33. Religion _is very hard, when when we have to know answers_ _by hear_
34. My worst _problem is math._
35. I am very _good in geography, his, music, writing, etc._
36. My childhood _is very happy._
37. Suicide _I will never commit_
38. I envy _my Mother and Father._
39. At night _I sleep._
40. My looks _are not to bad._
41. The dark _I am not afraid of._
42. My chief worry _is to keep calm._
43. When I _do school work in school, I get bored_
44. Fighting _I know how to do._
45. Children _are very nice._
46. My health _is very good._
47. I feel most proud of _having such a good Mother & Father_
48. Girls usually _talk to much in school._
49. Death _I hope will never be in my family._
50. My greatest ambition _is to get that marine raider camping set_ _for christ._

34

51. I like best _to march or play an instrument_.

52. My habits _are nervesness._

53. I try to get _my mother to get me that marine spider_ _camping set._

54. Love in my life _is easy because I get a lot of it from_ _father._

55. I get pleasure from _when I come home from school._

56. My teachers _are old._

57. I am sorry _for nothing._

58. At home _I'm very happy and any place where I go._

59. I feel hurt _never,_

60. Often I think _I'm smart._

61. I become embarrassed _never._

62. My head _is alright_

63. No one _hurts me._

64. I am ashamed _of nothing._

65. My education _is very good._

Write below anything that seems important to you. _____

_____

_____

_____

_____

_____

_____

_____

_____

Date of birth_____Age: Yrs._____Mos._____

Highest grade in school completed_____

Name of school or institution_____

Present occupation_____

35

The Rorschach Ink Blots

The administration of the Rorschach involves two steps. The first is called the Response Phase. Following a brief introduction each of the ten cards (labeled I-X) is handed to the examinee, always in the same order, then is asked, for each card, "What might this be?" Each of the examinee's responses to each card are recorded verbatim.

The second step is called the Inquiry Phase. Each card is again handed to the examinee, in the same numerical order, with the question "On this card you said _____. Can you show me where it is?" Further questions are asked about each of the responses to enable the examiner to accurately code them. This allows various aspects of each response (for example, whether the examinee used color or shading) to be reflected in the coding.

Only the aspect of coding, which indicates whether the subject used the whole blot *(W)* or just a specific details of the card *(D)*, is indicated on the responses given here. Space is left for psychologists to complete the coding.

Most examiners use common shorthand, such as "l.l." for "looks like" and "s.t." and "s.w." for "some thing" and "somewhat".

In reading the Rorschach responses it is probably best to read the first response to each card followed immediately by its inquiry and so on throughout the protocol.

Kenneth Bianchi'S Childhood Rorschach

K. B. 11 yrs male

RESPONSE	INQUIRY	SCORE
I. 1. It looks like the Canadian seal - I.I. there's a shield in the middle & two horses w/wings on the sides - have 'em on cigarettes	1. (whole) always see commercials with seal on it	W
II. 2. It I.I. half of a rhinoceros - two rhinoceroses - half of them	2. ears & horn & reflection in water (?) the horn mostly - short ears & flat head	D
3. top red ones I.I. some what like a butterfly	3. Butterfly w/wings folded up sideways & reflection on the water (?) way the wings come up	D
4. the bottom red one lks s.t. like a butterfly	4. Wild butterflies - yellowtails - no swallowtail - way they have fins sticking out (?) & the wings	D
	(one thing I didn't mention - toy tops w/the thing you push down - white part reminded me of that)	(DS)
III. 5. This I.I. a butler - two butlers & there's one big kettle & they're both carrying it & they're fighting about who is going to carry it	5. (?) their thin & they I.I. that - shape of head (?) water kettle - they're fighting over it	D
6. s.t. ike a butterfly in the middle	6. lks. sort of funny (?) so wide in the middle (?) the wings	D
7. there's s.t. like a seahorse over here	7. tail & head (?) like you see in a pet-shop	D
IV. 8. this I.I. some creature from outer space - from another planet	8. (?) (mentions parts) this I.I. eyebrows - I.I. he's mad	D
9. then it I.I. half a creature & then a dragon or dragon's head	9. this the dragon w/fire coming out of his nose - here ears and eyes	D

V. 10. Oh and this I.I. a butterfly - to me that's about all it I.I. is a butterfly	10. without these it would I.I. a butt-fly (?) looking at it from the bottom or top Dd
VI. 11, This one I.I. the top of it is part of a plant that's grown underneath the water & the bottom part - the big part - is the roots	11. These the roots only on a real one not so crooked - this the bulb & this part of the flower - this the stem growing more parts of the flower (?) just the shape D
VII. 12. This one I.I. two indians - little indians	12. feathers, nose, chin, eyes in here D I.I. they have a stick or s.t. behind they're back
13. & some kind of strange butter-fly on the bottom	13. well the wings (?) way shaped D (? b.fly) inside here - way butterflies are
VIII. 14. This I.I. two beavers - one beaver is walking on some rocks & the reflection of beaver walking on rocks is below	14. the ears, 4 legs - walking on rocks W in water (?) this the water line
IX. This one doesn't I.I. nothing to me - no (encouraged) nothing	Nothing (encouraged) no
X. 15. First of all the big one I.I. crab or seaweed	15. To me it I.I. a crab w/seaweed Dd stuck on him..
16. in the middle two small crabs	16. Round like crabs & have feelers D & some legs
17. & a knife in between 'em	17. I.I. separating the crabs (?) the D handle and blade (?) hunter's knife
18. & then I.I. s.k. of duck - baby duck in the middle & reflection in the in the water	18. leg, leg, tail, head (? baby) big one Dd wouldn't be that way (?) have no hair
	(s.t. else to me this I.I. upside down baseball player peaked hats - on team - probably scored home runs & holding a cup) (these I.I. collies w/o the dot would I.I. it - tail, leg, head - I.I. its jumping)

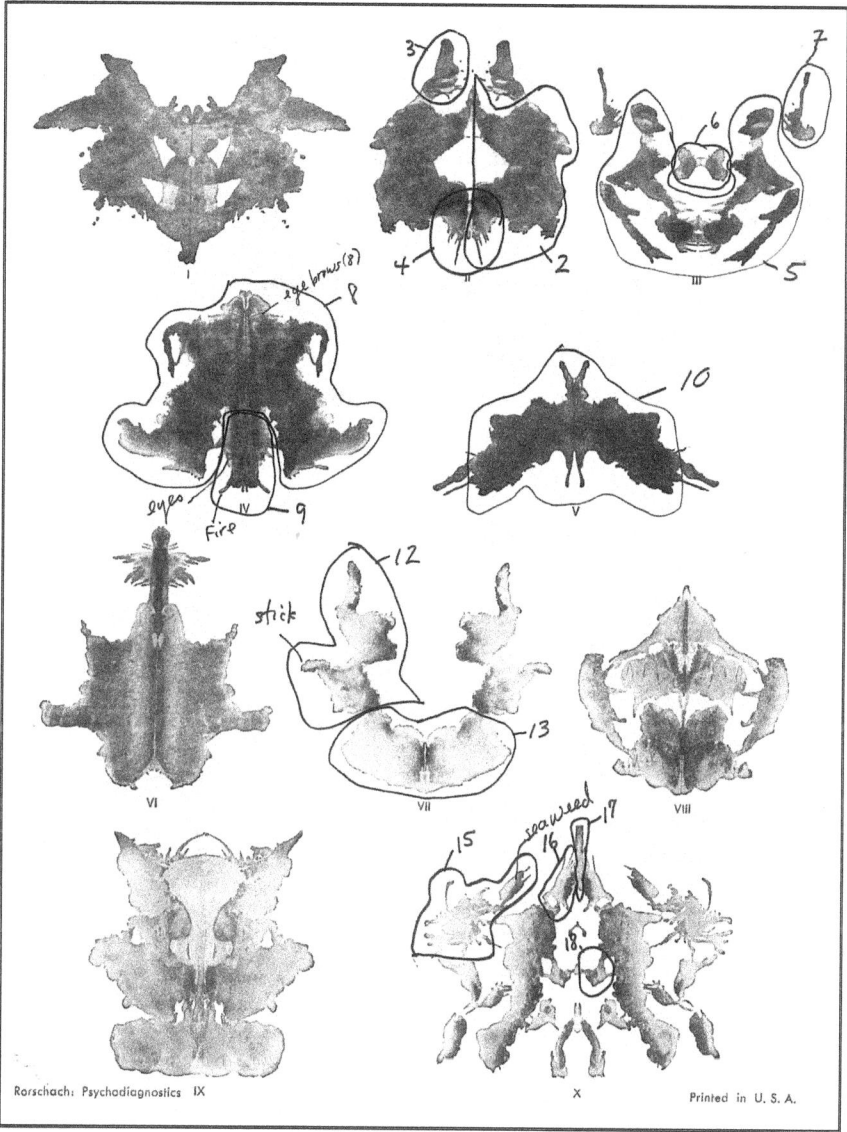

39

ADULT EVALUATION

Following Bianchi's arrest and confinement, a mental heath evaluation was conducted during which several psychological tests were administered. These included the Minnesota Personality Inventory, the California Psychological inventory, and two Rorschach Ink Blots. The first of the Rorschachs was administered to "Steve Walker" (while Bianchi was pretending to be hypnotized) and the second to Bianchi himself (not hypnotized) immediately afterwards.

The Minnesota Personality Inventory (MMPI)

This was administered on April 7, 1979. The following are the test profile and a copy of a computer generated interpretation of the findings.

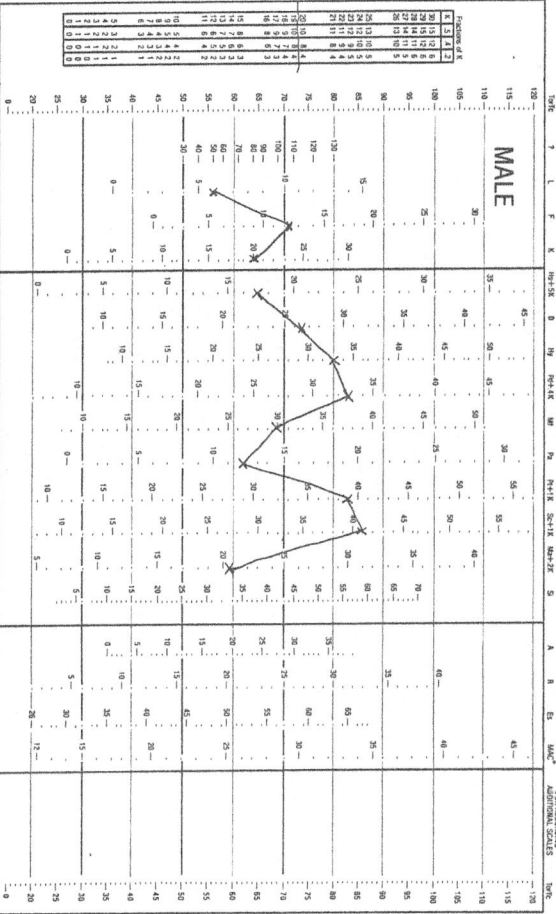

MINNESOTA MULTIPHASIC™
PERSONALITY INVENTORY
S.R. Hathaway and J.C. McKinley

PROFILE

MALE

NAME _K███ B ██████_
ADDRESS
OCCUPATION _____ DATE TESTED _4/9/79_
EDUCATION _____ AGE _27_
MARITAL STATUS _____ REFERRED BY _____

FOR RECORDING
ADDITIONAL SCALES

MMPI Code

_8473"2'516-9/_
_F'K-4/_

Scorer's Initials

	L	F	K	Hs+5K	D	Hy	Pd+4K	Mf	Pa	Pt+1K	Sc+1K	Ma+2K	Si
T+K	5.3	7.1	64.3	73.6	90.1	83.3	68.6	61.7	82.9	85.0	59.3	
Raw Score	6											
K to be added												

41

MMPI ANALYSIS

NAME: K. B.   AGE: 27   PRESENTING SYMPTOMS: NONE

This profile is valid. Individuals who obtain similar validity configurations
are often seen as displaying deficits in ego functions. A general negative
self-image and realization of need for psychological assistance are common
characteristics. Significant psychological problems are likely present and
delineation of their characteristics will be described below from the clinical
scales. A clearcut neurotic picture is, however, very unlikely.

Individuals who obtain similar profiles are often seen as introverted, unpredictable and peculiar in action and thought. Psychiatric patients who obtain this
pattern usually display clearly deviant behavior. These individuals experience
subtle communication problems; they have impaired empathy and find becoming
emotionally involved with others difficult. Similar individuals often act-out
in self-defeating ways and have difficulty evaluating social situations. They
are often angry with others but are unable to handle or express such feelings.
These patients should be carefully evaluated. They may have the potential for
antisocial or schizotypic behavior.

A history of schizoid adaptation is likely. Rule out paranoid trends and thought
disorder. Characterological an dpsychotic syndromes possible.

Moderate to severe levels of anxiety and tension make simple routine life tasks
difficult for this patient. Such individuals are often described as chronically
worrisome, apprehensive, rigid and meticulous. Phobias, compulsions and obsessive
ruminations are often characteristic

This patient's use of repression and denial is either ineffective or, at best,
wards off psychological discomfort at the cost of considerable psychic energy
and resultant rigidity. Functional physical complaints are likely. Such individuals are often described as insightless, immature, dependent, egocentric,
suggestible and demanding.

This patient is currently depressed, worried and pessimestic. Feelings of
self-depreciation and inadequacy are characteristic. Suicidal ideation and
tendencies should be ruled out, especially when behavioral depression is limited
or absent.

HIS INTEREST patterns are somewhat different from those of the average male
and may reflect a passive and noncompetitive personality. Those with more than
a high school education may have esthetic interests and may be seen by others as
sensitive and socially perceptive

IF K 65 T:

Though this appears to be a valid profile, the validity configuration suggests
an unusual response set. This patient is both admitting to significant
psychological problems and trying to appear psychological sound. This pattern
sometimes suggests the presence of an acute disturbance in an individual with
rather intact defenses. On the other hand , these results may suggest a severely
disturbed individual who is trying to be defensive but is not very successful. The
equilibrium between open expression of pathology and defensive control in these
individuals is both unstable and unpredictable.

The California Psychological Inventory (CPI)

The scores of four "persons" are displayed together on the CPI profile and then again on the subsequent sheets. These sheets provide a brief description of each of the dimensions measured.

The persons referred to as "K 1" and "Steve Walker", respectively, are Bianchi and his faked "other" personality. The individual referred to as "Ken 2" is also Bianchi who was administered this test by another examiner. "Billy" is the additional "other personality" who appeared when Bianchi was told by a forensic psychiatrist that most people with multiple personality disorders usually have more than one other personality.

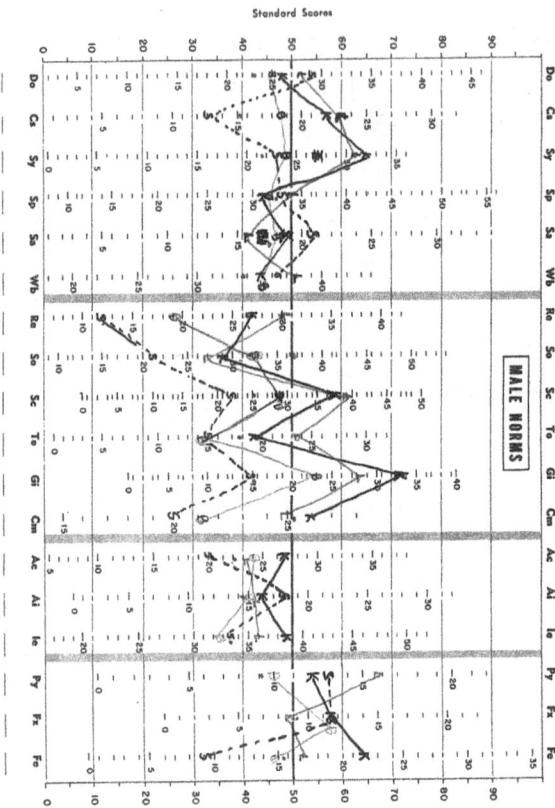

PROFILE SHEET FOR THE *California Psychological Inventory: MALE*

Name _____ Age _____ Date Tested _____

Other Information _____

Standard Scores

Do Cs Sy Sp Sa Wb Re So Sc To Gi Cm Ac Ai Ie Py Fx Fe

MALE NORMS

Standard Scores

Male Norms.

Notes:

K Ken I
L Ken II
S --- Steve

44

STANDARD GOUGH CPI SCORES

Scale	Test	5	10	15	20	25	30	35	40	45	50	55	60	65	70	75	80
DOM	Ken I	47.4							X→								
	Ken II	52.3									X	X					
	Steve	50.3									X						
	Billy	45.2								X							

DOM=Dominance: Identifies strong, dominant, influential individuals who can take the initiative and exercize leadership.

Scale	Test	5	10	15	20	25	30	35	40	45	50	55	60	65	70	75	80
CS	Ken I	55.9											X				
	Ken II	59.8												X			
	Steve	34.0						X									
	Billy	48.7									X						

CS=Capacity for Status: Appraises those qualities of ambition and self-assurance that underlie, and lead to, status.

Scale	Test	5	10	15	20	25	30	35	40	45	50	55	60	65	70	75	80
SY	Ken I	64.0												X			
	Ken II	62.6												X			
	Steve	46.2									X						
	Billy	48.2									X						

SY=Sociability: Identifies people with outgoing, sociable, participative temperments.

Scale	Test	5	10	15	20	25	30	35	40	45	50	55	60	65	70	75	80
SP	Ken I	43.2								X							
	Ken II	50.2										X					
	Steve	48.9									X						
	Billy	44.3								X							

SP=Social Pressence: Assesses poise, self-confidence and spontaneity in social interactions; High scorer may use and manipulate people.

Scale	Test	5	10	15	20	25	30	35	40	45	50	55	60	65	70	75	80
SA	Ken I	47.7									X						
	Ken II	41.0								X							
	Steve	54.9											X				
	Billy	45.8									X						

SA=Self-Acceptance: Assesses sense of self-worth, self-acceptance, and capacity for thinking and action.

Scale	Test	5	10	15	20	25	30	35	40	45	50	55	60	65	70	75	80
WB	Ken I	43.1								X							
	Ken II	50.5										X					
	Steve	47.1									X						
	Billy	43.4								X							

WB=Sense of Well Being: Measures sense of health and vitality. Validity scale with low scores indicating faking neurotic symptoms.

CPI SCALES ASSOCIATED WITH MULTIPLICITY

Scale	Test	5	10	15	20	25	30	35	40	45	50	55	60	65	70	75	80
#7	Ken I	72.4													X		
	Ken II	60.8									X						
	Steve	46.2							X								
	Billy	47.7							X								

Scale #7= Anxiety Score. Multiples score higher than normals.

#76	Ken K	42.3						X									
	Ken II	44.2						X									
	Steve	41.2						X									
	Billy	33.8				X											

Scale #76= Success in baseball (teamwork in competition) Multiples score lower than normals.

#145	Ken I	56.5								X							
	Ken II	71.4												X			
	Steve	56.9										X					
	Billy	43.3							X								

Scale #145= Evades: measures tendency to evade responsibility. Multiples score higher than normals.

#165	Ken I	49.2								X							
	Ken II	61.8										X					
	Steve	60.0										X					
	Billy	38.1				X											

Scale #165= Alcoholism (Holmes) Multiples score higher than normals.

DA	Ken I	63.7										X					
	Ken II	62.9										X					
	Steve	48.3								X							
	Billy	60.9										X					

DA= Dependency Average- measures tendency to lean on others for emotional suppoet. Multiples score lower than normals.

PPC	Ken I	4															
	Ken II	8															
	Steve	10															
	Billy	7															

PPC= Psychotic Point Count: Multiples score higher than normals.

41

STANDARD GOUGH CPI SCORES

Scale	Test	5	10	15	20	25	30	35	40	45	50	55	60	65	70	75	80
AC	Ken I 48.0									X							
	Ken II 41.9								X								
	Steve 33.9						X										
	Billy 42.4								X								

AC=Achievement via Conformance: Assesses factors associated with academic achievement due to internalized appreciation of structure and organization.

Scale	Test	5	10	15	20	25	30	35	40	45	50	55	60	65	70	75	80
AI	Ken I 44.0									X							
	Ken II 46.2									X							
	Steve 49.2										X						
	Billy 41.7								X								

AI=Achievement via Independence: Predicts academic achievement where independence of thought, creativity, and self-actualization is rewarded.

Scale	Test	5	10	15	20	25	30	35	40	45	50	55	60	65	70	75	80
IE	Ken I 49.7										X						
	Ken II 44.0									X							
	Steve 38.2								X								
	Billy 36.8							X									

IE=Intellectual Efficiency: Measures personality items correlated with standard IQ tests.

Scale	Test	5	10	15	20	25	30	35	40	45	50	55	60	65	70	75	80
PY	Ken I 54.6											X					
	Ken II 67.8														X		
	Steve 58.6												X				
	Billy 47.6									X							

PY=Psychological Mindedness: Identifies those interested in, and responsive to, the inner needs, motives and experiences of others.

Scale	Test	5	10	15	20	25	30	35	40	45	50	55	60	65	70	75	80
FX	Ken I 57.6												X				
	Ken II 49.8										X						
	Steve 57.7												X				
	Billy 57.7												X				

FX=Flexibility: Identifies those who are flexible, adaptible, and even somewhat changeable in their thinking, behavior and temperment

Scale	Test	5	10	15	20	25	30	35	40	45	50	55	60	65	70	75	80
FE	Ken I 64.5													X			
	Ken II 52.8											X					
	Steve 32.4						X										
	Billy 46.7									X							

FE=Femininity: Measures psychological femininity, not physical sexual differences or homosexual tendencies. Low=macho.

47

The "Steve Walker" Rorschach

This was administered while Bianchi was pretending to be hypnotized after "Steve" was "called out".

Please note the absence of an Inquiry Phase and the examiner's note concerning this in the upper right hand corner.

S.W. YOUNG MAN

(No inquiry done because subject constantly threatened examiner and became quiet violent at the slightest suggestion of questioning his first response.)

RESPONSE	INQUIRY	SCORE
I. 5" 1. Two elephants fucking each other. (Anything else? Fuck no.		W
II. 3" 2. Somebody eating out a cherry broad (?) Don't you know what that means man? Do I have to spell it out for you .		W
III. 5" 3. Two guys humping a cunt man.		D1
4. Don't know. These things l.l. seahorses.		W
IV. 3" 5. A giant man. See his dick.		W
V. 5" 6. Two broads lying beside each other.	(one on each side)	Dd99
VI. 12" 7. A big dick.		D6
VII. 8" 8. It l.l. Siamese twins, but its not. It's two broads getting it on.	(Dd22 x 2)	W
VIII. 15" 9. Some cat got hit by a car.		W
IX. 21" 10. Looks like an abortion.		W
X. 16" 11. Looks like a bunch of ink thrown on a card.		W

The Bianchi Adult Rorschach

Immediately after "Steve" had completed the Rorschach, Bianchi was "called back" and the test was again administered by the same examiner.

COMMENT

The Rorschach protocols of Bianchi and "Steve" were sent to three highly experienced and respected psychologists well known for their expertise with this test. One of them interpreted the tests to be from two different people or from two personalities, should they be from one person. The other two psychologists interpreted the protocols as coming from the same individual, in spite of the great differences in the content of the responses. They based their conclusion on the underlying similarities in the cognitive style in both records.

K. Age 27

RESPONSE	INQUIRY	SCORE
I. 7"		
1. Two people dancing. Like in a discotheque.	1. Arms, legs, kicking motion. middle.	D
2. L.I. a game we use to play. London Bridge. *Person here in the middle, people on each side.*	2.	W
II. 4"		
3. L.I. two dogs fighting over the same bone.	3. Nose, shape, fur hair.	D
Those red parts don't I.I. anything.	(color denial)	
III. 15"		
4. I used to work at a country club--parcel parties. L.I. when we carried out large baskets. Two men carrying a basket.	4. Men wearing vests--perhaps.	W
5. Thing in the middle I.i. a butterfly.	5. Because of shape.	D
IV. 5"		
6. L.I. a Got (?) tree in California. As your just starting to go into it and looking up. (He seems to mean a tree like a large redwood.)	6. From an angle. I do drawings. The distance it narrows. (doesn't include the middle)	D
7. This one part here I.I. the head of a snail.	7. Tentacles. It has a sort soft look. (shading)	D
V. 5"		
8. A moth or butterfly. I use to collect them as a child. Monarch.	8. A section of the wings like a Monarch. (?) More like a moth.	W

51

RESPONSE	INQUIRY	SCORE
VI. 10"		
9. L.I. a steamboat in the water. Reflection. Propeller in the rear. Here's a wave.	9.	W
VII. 7"		
10. My mom used to tell me a story. L.I. the two little indians facing each other.	10. Feather, nose, little bodies. Tomahawk between them.	D
11. L.I. a moth.	11. Body in center. A little small. Because of shape.	D
VIII. 5"		
12. This l.l. some kind of animal. A mountain lion or leopard. Roughage around shore.	12. Body could be a mountain lion. Head, however, i.i. the head of a bear. A rock formation. Shape, water, reflection.	D
IX. 21" (much card turning)		
13. Can I break it down? (Up to you.) This one part down the middle i.i. a spinal cord.	13. Rib cage.	D
14. This pink l.l. an unborn fetus in the womb.	14. Head is larger than the body. Two of them. The eyes forming. Seems like twin fetuses. Light-dark. Shading.	D
15. L.I. Asia--like a continent.	15. Dark area could be mountains. (?) This blue area.	D
X. 26" (much card turning)		
16. L.I. two men mountain climbing. They could be helping each other.	16.	D
17. This figure up here is a girl swinging from a rope swing,	17. Green area.	D

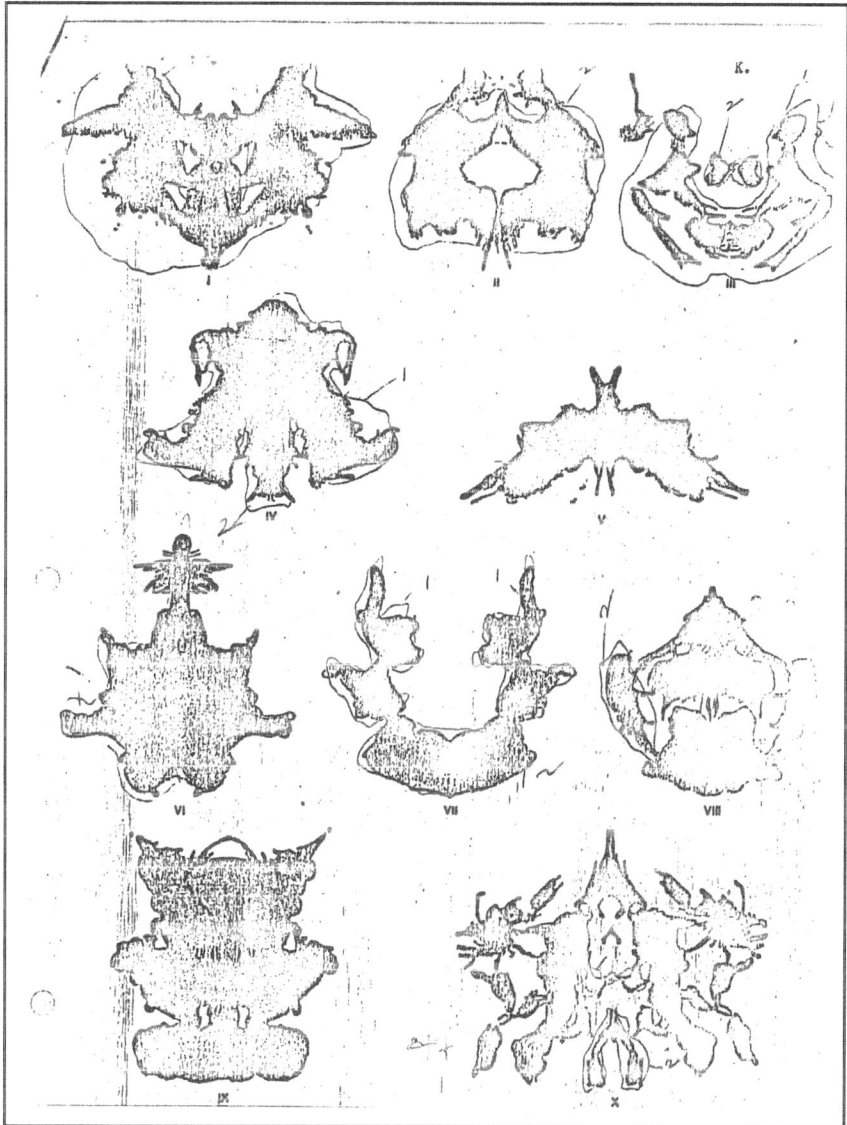

53

IV

—∿—

COMPARISON OF THE CHILDHOOD
AND ADULT RORSCHACHS

Of all the tests taken by Bianchi the Rorschach Ink Blots was the only one administered to him both as a child and as an adult. For a separate project in 2003 the author and a colleague, Dr. Sharon Hamilton, made a statistical comparison of the two test protocols.

We each first scored the protocols independently using the Exner Comprehensive System (Exner 2001). We then identified those variables which differed by at least one standard deviation either above or below there respective mean scores at each of their respective age levels. Above and below the mean were both included because the absence of certain types of responses are as important in Rorschach interpretation as their presence.

Eight variables met these criteria: four were below their mean score and four were above their mean score.

The four variables which were found to be below the mean at both the younger and older ages:

1ˢᵗ below: This variable is the total number of responses (coded *R).*

The number of responses given at both ages, although meeting the criterion of one standard deviation below the mean, were each greater than the minimum of 14 considered to be sufficient for interpretive validity (Exner, 2001 p. 7). Thus, there is little significant to be attributable to this variable.

2ⁿᵈ below: This variable is the number of animal responses seen in motion (coded *FM).*

The low number of animal movement responses in both data sets is also of limited interpretive value. In the Exner system it is one of several variables which when combined with others are used in evaluating the subject's stress tolerance. In both records these additional variables did not meet the criterion of being being below their mean score.

3ʳᵈ below: This variable is the number of responses that include naming color of the object seen (coded *FC* and *CF).*

At both ages there was an absence of color responses. In all of the various coding approaches that have been used with the Rorschach, responses involving the color aspects of the cards have been seen as important. Beginning with Dr. Hermann Rorschach color responses have been interpreted as relating to the use of affect (Searls, 2017 pp.134-135). Scores of zero color responses, as seen in both records at each age, indicate an avoidance or absence of responding to the emotional aspect of the cards. This suggests either not feeling anything in response to the blots or a need to keep feelings under considerable control (Exner, 2001 p.330).

4ᵗʰ below: This variable is obtained by assigning weights to responses that involve a colored objects or colored animals (coded *WeightedSumC*).

This value (zero at both ages), when compared to the number of movement responses (M), yields what is referred to as an "introverted" style. Such a style indicates a preference "to keep feelings at a more peripheral level during problem solving and decision making" (Exner, 2001 p.192-193).

Four of the variables were found to be above the mean at both ages:

1st above: This variable is the percentage of responses receiving a form quality score of 'unusual' (coded *Xu%-).* Each response is rated as to how well the form of the percept seen fits the shape of the part of the blot used.

A high number of such responses, although having appropriate form quality, are judged to be unusual and unconventional. As such, they indicate behavior which disregards social expectation (Exner, 2001 p. 189).

2nd above: This variable is the difference between the achieved organizational score and the expected organizational score, given the number of responses involving organizational activity (coded *Zd-*).

According to Exner (2001, p.257) a score on this variable that is "greater than +3 ... indicates an enduring trait-like characteristic to avoid being careless and this motivates them to exert more effort than is necessary to scan the features of a situation."

3rd above: This is a variable calculated by the formula "3r+(2)/R" where "r" is the number of responses involving seeing the object as a reflexion, "(2)" is the number of responses involving pairs, and "R" is the total number of responses (coded *Egocentricity Index*).

A high score, seen at both the younger and older ages, "indicates an excessive involvement with the self" (Exner 2001 p. 256).

4th above: This is the sum of all the responses which involve seeing the object as a reflection (coded *Fr+rF*).

The presence of a high number of reflection responses in connection with an above average *Egocentricity Index* indicates that a "narcissistic-like feature is strongly imbedded in the psychology of the person" (Exner, 2001. p. 257).

The findings indicate the presence at both the ages of 11 years and 27 years the following four characteristic personalty traits:

- the presence of the need to control emotions;

- cautiousness in assessing the environment but unconventional in its interpretation;

- the avoidance or absence of feeling; and

- a significant degree of narcissism,

The findings also indicate that these personality characteristics have their origin prior to adolescence and remain central features of the personality at least through early adulthood.

One cannot but notice that some of them at least are among those that are traditionally associated with psychopathic personality disorders.

Looking beyond the Rorschach coded variables one can find other interesting parallels. At both ages, eleven and twenty-seven, Bianchi gave essentially the same response to Rorschach Card VII: "two little Indians". Although some versions of "Indians" is a common response to this card, his exact wording is noteworthy;

The only nonsexual or non-aggressive response given by "Steve" (actually Bianchi) to the Rorschach was precisely the same as that given by him at age eleven, both to Card III: 'these look like seahorses". Again, although a common response to this card, the exact wording was used.

Looking at his test responses, other than on the Rorschach, one notes Bianchi's continuing attraction to the police and uniforms (see Draw-a-Person p. 28). This kind of interest is a fairly common characteristic among serial killers (Vronsky, 2004 p. 310).

V

END NOTES

Looking at the history of serial killers, whether they acted alone or with others, is interesting but not very revealing. A perusal of the many internet sites dealing with serial murderers uncovers the existence of a variety of combinations in addition to the lone slayer. The latter make up the majority of serial killers but one also finds pairs, trios, and even larger groups including some involving whole families. Among the pairs there are quite a few male and female partners (many married) and also some sets of females. But the majority of duo serial killers consist of adult men who became acquainted quite by chance. It probably was only a matter of time before they discovered their mutual extreme misogyny.

Angelo Buono's cruel mistreatment of women had a long history before Bianchi came on the scene. Contrarily, Kenneth Bianchi was somewhat of a "poster boy" for the Freudian "Madonna-whore" complex. He treated women he met in every day life, and especially those he found attractive, with respect and deference. But he took to his elder cousin's attitude toward other women quite easily, even with enthusiasm.

Both of them had many psychopathic tendencies but each had been expressing them in their own ways. Neither of them had ever been charged with or even suspected of murder. But it was only two years after they came together that the rampage took place. Perhaps, even probably, they needed each other: Buono providing the setting, the opportunity and "mature" caution; Bianchi providing the youthful carelessness, encouragement and excitement. It is possible that neither would have become a murderer had they not come together as they did.

The previous chapter indicates that certain personality tendencies have their beginnings prior to the start of the teen years and continue to be expressed in early adulthood. But, obviously, subsequent life events influence their final place and importance in the total personalty make-up. Bianchi's late adolescence and early adulthood were characterized by failure in both the crucial areas of love and work. How shortcomings in these two major areas of "growing up", as well as the other myriad happenings that took place, played a role in making him what he became will remain unknown. We can only achieve a limited understanding of how this frightened child became a serial killer.

～～

It is hoped that this presentation of the psychological evaluations of a single person helps in the understanding of him and of others like him. It is also hoped that this case study makes some contribution to the important place of the idiographic approach in the science of psychology.

BIBLIOGRAPHY

Exner, John E. The Rorschach: A Comprehensive System, Volume 2: Interpretation, 2nd Edition, 1991, John Wiley & Sons, New York.

O'Brien, Darcy Two of a Kind: The Hillside Stranglers, 1985, New American Library, New York.

Roberts, Naomi The Hillside Stranglers, 2016 (self published).

Schwarz, Ted The Hillside Strangler: A Murderer's Mind, 1981, Doubleday and Company, New York.

Searls, Damion The Ink Blots: Hermann Rorschach, His Iconic Test, and the Power of Seeing, 2017, Crown Publishing, New York.

Vronsky, Peter Serial Killers: The Method and Madness of Monsters, 2004, The Penguin Group, New York.

Appendix A

LETTER FROM
ATTORNEY DEAN BRET TO THE AUTHOR

BRETT, BRINN, DAUGERT & ERICKSON
ATTORNEYS AT LAW
308 NORTH COMMERCIAL
P. O. BOX 816
BELLINGHAM, WASHINGTON 98225

DEAN BRETT
STEVEN BRINN
LARRY DAUGERT
JOHN ERICKSON

TELEPHONE 733-0212
AREA CODE 206

October 29, 1979

Robert M. Dowling, Ph.D.
Park Place
1545 West 38th Street
Erie, Pennsylvania 16508

Dear Dr. Dowling:

Thank you for your assistance in the case of Kenneth A. Bianchi.
Enclosed please find a check for your services.

I regret that we were unable to try this interesting psychiatric
defense but when the states of California and Washington agreed
to drop 12 death penalty counts, we had no alternative but to
accept their offer.

I am also enclosing a copy of the psychiatric reports submitted
by the six experts appointed by the court in this case. You will
note that four of them found that Ken Bianchi was not faking and
that he was a dissociative reaction. These included the two appointed by the defense and the two independent psychiatrists
appointed by the court. The two psychiatrists, Orne and Faerstein,
appointed by the prosecuting attorney opined that Ken was "faking"
and a sociopath.

Your reports done at the DePaul Clinic were submitted to the court
as part of a complete chronological history. That chronological
history and all of the audio and video tapes of all the examinations
of the psychiatrists are now a matter of public record so we have
put together for the scientific community what I believe is the
most complete documentation of a dissociative reaction it's seen.

Again, that you for your assistance.

Sincerely,

BRETT, BRINN, DAUGERT & ERICKSON

By Dean Brett

DB:pg
Enc.

Appendix B

DOCUMENTS CONCERNING THE "STEVE WAKER" INCIDENT

To whom this may concern:

I would appreciate it if you could forward the fully completed diplomas EXCEPT for my name. I have at an additional expense retained a cal - igrapher that will print my name in a fancy script of my choice. If this request cannot be honored please return the enclosed M.O..

Yours Truly

Thomas Steven Walker

T.S. Walker M.A.

Master of Arts
Pepperdine University, Los Angeles, CA
Graduated August 1977   Major General Psychology

AUGUST 7, 1977

Bachelor of Arts
California State University, Northridge, CA
Graduated May 1975   Major Psychology
HONORS   Magna Cum Laude   *MAY 30, 1975*

Send all replys to: Thomas S. Walker
c/o Mrs. K. Bianchi
610 S. Verdugo Road #31
Glendale, California 91205

ENCLOSED $90.00

CR PT	COURSE NO	TITLE		UNITS ATTEMPTED	UNITS PASSED	GRADE	GRADE POINTS
		Los Angeles Valley College	U.S. Air Force 8/61-9/70				
		Military Credit: U.S. Air Force 9/66-1/73					
SPRG	1973	732 0060		906592	61.0	61.0	179.0
PSY	310	BEHAV DISORDEHS		4.0	4.0	B	12.0
PSY	320	STAT METH PSY RES		4.0	4.0	B	12.0
PSY	320S	RES SEM STAT METH		2.0	2.0	B	6.0
SOC	202	SOC ANALYSIS		3.0	3.0	B	9.0
CUM	12.0	79.0	36.0 3.00 BAL +	12.0	12.0	3.00	36.0
FALL	1973	732 0060		234540			
PSY	370	DYN INDIVID BEHAV		3.0	3.0	A	12.0
PSY	370S	RES SEM IND BEHAV		2.0	2.0	A	8.0
PSY	454	CLINICAL PSYCH		4.0	4.0	A	16.0
CUM	21.0	88.0	72.0 3.43 BAL +	9.0	9.0	4.00	36.0
SPRG	1974	732 0360		225970			
PHIL	497	PHIL ISS IN PSYCH		3.0	3.0	B	9.0
PSY	321	EXPERIMENTAL PSY		3.0	3.0	A	12.0
PSY	321S	RES SEM EXP PSY		2.0	2.0	A	8.0
PSY	451	SEX ROLE STERED		4.0	4.0	A	16.0
CUM	33.0	109.0	117.0 3.55 BAL +	12.0	12.0	3.75	45.0
FALL	1974	732 0060		243000			
PSY	313	DEVELOPMENTAL PSY		3.0	3.0	A	12.0
PSY	313S	RES SEM DEVEL PSY		2.0	2.0	A	8.0
PSY	356	INDUSTRIAL PSYCH		3.0	3.0	B	8.0
PSY	436	THEOR PERSONALITY		4.0	4.0	A	12.0
CUM	45.0	112.0	158.0 3.51 BAL	12.0	12.0	4.00	41.0
SPRG	1975	732 0060		236120			
PSY	245	CONT SOC ISSUES		3.0	3.0	A	12.0
PSY	318	SENS + PERCEPTION		3.0	3.0	A	12.0
PSY	318S	RES SEM SENS PERC		2.0	2.0	B	8.0
PSY	425	HIST + PERSPEC		4.0	4.0	A	16.0
CUM	57.0	124.0	206.0 3.61 BAL +	12.0	12.0	4.00	48.0
		DEANS LIST	92.0				

BA 5/30/75 (Magna Cum Laude) Psychology

WALKER THOMAS S

Brenda,

I just had to write this letter, because I'm very dissappointed. I received the diplomas and I can't believe my eyes. The names you did aren't even centered, and on one of the diplomas the name wasn't even.. Those diplomas cost me $45. each to have a company duplicate them after almost a 2 month wait because they had to verify my school records. I have no display use for my diplomas in the condition they're in. $90.00 down the drain. If you couldn't do a real quality job I wish you would've returned the untouched documents to me. If you don't believe me on their cost you can call Diploma Service Co., Marina Del Rey. I can't take the $90. loss so I'm sorry, but unless I voluntarily recover the $90. in damages I'm afraid I'm going to have to have my attorney recover the damages, which having been contacted he said he would do so at my request, plus he will legally collect from you in court for his costs and my inconvenience. I explained their value and left them in your care, and you did not do a good job. Sorry.

K. Bianchi
3207 W. Maplewood
Bellingham, WA
98225

P.S. I'm sorry but if I don't get any satisfaction I'm afraid I'll have to report you to the Bureau of Consumer Affairs for conducting a business without a liscence, I'm sure the IRS would be interested also.

67

www.ingramcontent.com/pod-product-compliance
Lightning Source LLC
Chambersburg PA
CBHW052105270326
41931CB00012B/2894